INTERNATIONAL EXPRESS

PRE-INTERMEDIATE

Pocket Book

Liz Taylor

OXFORD UNIVERSITY PRESS

Contents

Student's Book Unit	Grammar	Page
	List of grammar terms	1
1	Present Simple	2
1	Question words	2
2	Present Continuous	3
3	Past Simple	4
4	Comparative and superlative adjectives	5
5	Mass and count nouns	6
5	*Some, any, a lot of, much, many*	6
6,7	Present Perfect Simple	7
7	Present Perfect Continuous	8
7	*since* and *for*	8
8	Future: *going to*	9
8	Future: Present Continuous	9
9	Future: *will*	10
9	1st Conditional	11
10	2nd Conditional	12
11	Modal verbs	13
12	The Passive	14
10	Prepositions: time, place, and direction	15
3,6,7	List of irregular verbs	16

	Social English	
1	Meeting people	17
2	Telephoning	18
3	Welcoming a visitor	18
4	Staying at a hotel	19
5	At a restaurant	19
6	Making arrangements	20
7	Opinions and suggestions	20
8	Invitations	21
9	Offers and requests	21
10	Asking for information	22
11	Social responses	22
12	Saying goodbye	23

	Other useful information	
	Asking for help	23
	Business correspondence	24
	American English	26
	Mathematical terms	27
	Countries and nationalities	28
	List of phonetic symbols	28
	Grammar timelines	29

GRAMMAR

List of grammar terms

An **adjective**	describes a noun – people, places, things, events, etc. a *beautiful* city, an *enjoyable* holiday, *interesting* people, *terrible* news
An **adverb**	adds information, for example, about when, where, or how something happens. She wrote the report *yesterday*. He's waiting *outside*. Please drive *slowly*.
An **adverb of frequency**	describes how often something happens. I *always* play tennis in the summer. I'm *rarely* late for work.
An **auxiliary verb**	(*be*, *do*, and *have*) is used with other verbs to make tenses and passive forms. She *is* working in Geneva. Where *did* you go? The window *has been* broken.
The **infinitive**	is the base form of the verb (*come*, *go*, etc.). It is used with or without *to*. It's good *to meet* you. I'd like *to introduce* you to a friend. I must *go* now.
A **modal verb**	is a verb like *might*, *can*, and *should*. We use them to express possibility, ask permission, give advice, etc. She *might* arrive late. *Can* I use your phone? You *should* see a doctor.
A **noun**	is a person, place, thing, or idea. a *journalist*, an *office*, *books*, *beauty*
A **preposition**	indicates place, time, direction, etc. I live *in* a flat. He walks *to* his office every day. They begin work *at* 8 o'clock.
A **pronoun**	takes the place of a noun. The restaurant is very good but *it* is expensive. Do *you* know Sue? I saw *her* at the theatre last night.
A **verb**	expresses an action or a state. He *writes* for a magazine. I *speak* French. She *didn't enjoy* the film.

Present Simple

Positive		Negative		
I You We They	work.	I You We They	don't (do not)	work.
He She It	works.	He She It	doesn't (does not)	

Question			Short answer		
Do	I you we they	work?	Yes,	I you we they	do.
			No,		don't.
Does	he she it		Yes,	he she it	does.
			No,		doesn't.

Use	Examples
Long-term situations	*I live in Madrid.* *Where does she work?*
Habits and routines	*I travel to work by car.* *How often do you play golf?*
Feelings and opinions	*She doesn't like her work.* *I agree with you.*
Facts	*The journey takes 30 minutes.* *It costs £150.*

Question words

Where *do you live?* — In Rome.
What *do you do at weekends?* — I usually play golf.
When *do they take their holiday?* — In July or August.
Which *magazine does James write for?* — Wine and Dine.
How *do you travel to work?* — By car.
How often *do you make business trips?* — About twice a month.
Whose *book is this?* — It's mine.
Who/(Whom) *do you visit in London?* — I visit my sister.
Who *arrives at work first?* — Anna does.

- *Whom* is very formal, and is not used very often.

Present Continuous

Positive			Negative		
I	'm (am)		I	'm not (am not)	
He She It	's (is)	working.	He She It	isn't (is not)	working.
You We They	're (are)		You We They	aren't (are not)	

Question			Short answer		
Am	I		Yes,	I	am.
			No,		'm not.
Is	he she it	working?	Yes,	he she it	is.
			No,		isn't.
Are	you we they		Yes,	you we they	are.
			No,		aren't.

Use	Examples
Actions happening now	*He's talking on the phone at the moment.* *They're having lunch with a customer.*
Temporary situations or actions	*Jeans are selling well this season.* *I'm not travelling on business this month.* *Which hotel are you staying at?*

- A dictionary tells you when the final consonant doubles (*travel*, *travelling*), and when we leave out the final *e* (*make*, *making*).

Past Simple

Positive			Negative			
I You He She It We They	started rang*	yesterday.	I You He She It We They	didn't (did not)	start ring*	yesterday.

Question				Short answer		
Did	I you he she it we they	start ring*	yesterday?	Yes, No,	I you he she it we they	did. didn't.

*See the list of irregular verbs on p. 16.

Use	Examples
Finished situations and actions in the past	*I lived in Rome for two years.* *He flew to America last week.* *They didn't come to the party.* *Where did you spend your last holiday?*

- We often use the Past Simple with finished time phrases like *yesterday, last week, an hour ago*.
- Regular verbs in the Past Simple end in *-ed*. A dictionary tells you when the consonant doubles (Group 3), and when the *-y* changes to *-i* (Group 4).

Group 1	work worked	play played	wait waited
Group 2	live lived	smile smiled	close closed
Group 3	stop stopped	travel travelled	plan planned
Group 4	study studied	worry worried	try tried

- When the infinitive ends in a /d/ or a /t/ sound (*attend* /ə'tend/, *visit* /'vɪzɪt/), we pronounce the *-ed* ending as /ɪd/ (*attended* /ə'tendɪd/, *visited* /'vɪzɪtɪd/).

See Grammar timelines on p. 29.

Comparative and superlative adjectives

Form	Adjective	Comparative		Superlative	
One syllable	long few hot	longer fewer hotter		the	longest fewest hottest
Two syllables ending in -y	easy happy	easier happier		the	easiest happiest
Two or more syllables	famous crowded expensive	more	famous crowded expensive	the most	famous crowded expensive
Irregular adjectives	good bad much/many little far	better worse more less farther/ further		the	best worst most least farthest/ furthest

Use	Examples
We use *than* after a comparative adjective.	London is bigger than Paris. The Ritz is more expensive than the Hilton.
Much can come before the comparative to add emphasis.	He is much younger than his brother. Tokyo is much more expensive than Rome.
We use *the* before a superlative adjective.	Canary Wharf is the tallest building in London.
As ... as shows something is the same or equal.	Greece is as sunny as Spain. I am as happy as you are.
Not as ... as shows something isn't the same or equal.	Italy isn't as big as France.

- One syllable adjectives ending with one vowel and a consonant double the consonant: *big   bigger   biggest*
   fat   fatter   fattest
- This doesn't happen when the consonant is *-w* or *-y*:
   new   newer   newest
   grey   greyer   greyest

Mass and count nouns

Mass nouns	Use	Examples
	Mass nouns have no plural form. We do not use *a* or *an* with them. We use them with a singular verb form.	*They want some information.* *I don't like music.* *This machinery is expensive.*

Count nouns	Use	Examples
	Count nouns have a singular and plural form. We use them with *a* and *an*. We use them with singular and plural verb forms.	*This machine is expensive.* *Did you have a good trip?* *These machines are expensive.*

Some nouns are both mass and count.

Mass/ Count nouns	Use	Examples
	Mass (general meaning)	*James writes about wine.* *She has a lot of experience of the travel industry.*
	Count (specific meaning)	*He's writing a book about the wines of Italy.* *I had some amusing experiences on my last holiday.*

some, any, a lot of, much, many

	Use	Examples
some	With mass and count nouns in positive sentences In offers and requests	*I bought some tea.* *She made some appointments.* *Would you like some coffee?* *Could I have some information?*
any	With mass and count nouns in negative sentences In questions	*I didn't buy any apples.* *He didn't spend any money.* *Did they give you any help?* *Do you have any questions?*
a lot of/ lots of	With mass and count nouns in positive sentences	*There's a lot of traffic today.* *There are a lot of cars in the city centre.* *Lots of people go jogging in the park.*
much	With mass nouns in negative sentences, and in questions	*We haven't got much luggage.* *I don't have much time.* *How much paper do you need?*
many	With count nouns in negative sentences, and in questions	*We haven't got many suitcases.* *She didn't have many meetings.* *How many people did you invite?*
	In positive sentences	*Many people are on holiday this week.*

- In positive sentences, *a lot of/lots of* is more common than *many*.
- We can use *a lot of/lots of* in negative sentences and in questions.
- *Lots of* is mostly used in informal spoken English.

Present Perfect Simple

Positive			Negative		
I You We They	've (have)	arrived. begun.	I You We They	haven't (have not)	arrived. begun.
He She It	's (has)		He She It	hasn't (has not)	

Question			Short answer		
Have	I you we they	arrived? begun?	Yes, No,	I you we they	have. haven't.
Has	he she it		Yes, No,	he she it	has. hasn't.

Use	Examples
Finished experiences in your life up to now	She's lived in China and Japan. He's had experience of marketing. Have you ever been to Brazil?
Recent situations and actions in a time up to now	We've reduced prices. Corporate business has increased significantly. Have you had a holiday this year?
Situations that started in the past and still continue	He's been an architect since 1992. She's had a translation agency for ten years. How long have you known her?
Past actions in a time up to now where we give the quantity	She's designed a lot of fashion items for Burberrys. How many letters have you written?

- *gone to* or *been to?*
  Ann's **gone to** New York, means she's in New York now, or she's on her way there.
  Ann's **been to** New York, means she's not in New York now. Her visit is over.

- Contracted forms
  In spoken English, we usually say *I've, you've, he's*, etc.
  In formal, written English we normally use *I have, you have, he has*, etc.

- For information on *yet, just, already*, see p. 26.
  See Grammar timelines on p. 29

Present Perfect Continuous

Positive			Negative		
I You We They	've (have)	been working.	I You We They	haven't (have not)	been working.
He She It	's (has)		He She It	hasn't (has not)	

Question			Short answer		
Have	I you we they	been working?	Yes, No,	I you we they	have. haven't.
Has	he she it		Yes, No,	he she it	has. hasn't.

Use	Examples
Actions that began in the past and continue to the present	We've been producing pens since the 1980s. He's been living here for five years. How long have you been learning English?
Actions that began in the past and have just stopped	You look very tired. Have you been working? I'm hot because I've been running.

- The Present Perfect Continuous and Simple are similar in meaning. The form we use often depends on whether we are more interested in the action or its result.
  I've been fixing the car. (My hands are dirty.)
  I've fixed the car. (Now I can drive to work.)

- We use the Present Perfect Continuous to say *how long*.
  They've been interviewing people since 10 a.m.
  She's been writing letters all morning.
  We use the Present Perfect Simple to say *how many*.
  They've interviewed nine people.   *She's written five letters.*

for and *since*

Use	Examples		Use	Examples	
With a period of time	for	three days five hours a month ten minutes a long time ages	With a point in time	since	Tuesday 8 August 4 o'clock last summer 1982 I last saw you

Future: *going to*

Positive			Negative		
I	'm (am)	going to begin.	I	'm not (am not)	going to begin.
He She It	's (is)		He She It	isn't (is not)	
You We They	're (are)		You We They	aren't (are not)	

Question			Short answer		
Am	I	going to begin?	Yes,	I	am.
			No,		'm not.
Is	he she it	going to begin?	Yes,	he she it	is.
			No,		isn't.
Are	you we they	going to begin?	Yes,	you we they	are.
			No,		aren't.

Use	Examples
Future plans, intentions, and decisions	We're going to buy a new car soon. When are you going to have a holiday? I'm not going to have lunch today.
Future actions we feel certain about because of what we can see now	The sky's very dark. I'm sure it's going to rain. Look out! That car's going to hit you!

- With *come* and *go*, we usually use the Present Continuous.
  I'm **going** on holiday soon.
  Are they **coming** by car on Saturday?

Future: Present Continuous

For Present Continuous form see p. 3.

Use	Examples
Fixed future arrangements	I'm flying to Tokyo at 10 a.m. tomorrow. When is the President arriving? I'm not playing golf this weekend.

Future: will

Positive			Negative		
I You He She It We They	'll (will)	arrive.	I You He She It We They	won't (will not)	arrive.

Question			Short answer		
Will	I you he she it we they	arrive?	Yes, No,	I you he she it we they	will. won't.

Use	Examples
Future facts and predictions	*The new hotel will cost £10 million.* *The construction work won't start until next year.* *How many jobs will there be?*
Decisions made at the time of speaking	*I'll give you the report today.* *Hold on a minute, I'll write down your phone number.*

1st Conditional

if + Present Simple, *will* + infinitive (without *to*)

Positive	Negative
If they offer me the job, I'll accept it. We'll have a lot of work if we get the contract.	If you don't study more, you'll fail your exam. They won't visit us if they're very busy. If they don't leave now, they won't arrive on time.

Question	Short answer
Will you buy a new car if you have the money? If you ask him, will he tell you? What will he do if his plane arrives late?	Yes, I will. No, he won't. —

Use	Examples
Future possibilities and their results	*If the proposal becomes a reality, it will revolutionize train travel in Europe.* *If the weather is bad, the train will arrive before the plane.*

- The *if* clause can come before or after the main clause. When the *if* clause comes first, we usually put a comma between it and the main clause.
  If the meeting is successful, we'll sign the contract.
  We'll sign the contract if the meeting is successful.
- For things we are certain will happen, we use *when* not *if*.
  When *he returns from the USA, he'll contact you.* (We know he will return.)
  We'll leave **when** *we finish the work.* (We know we will finish the work.)

2nd Conditional

if + Past Simple, *would* + infinitive (without *to*)

Positive	Negative
If I had more time, I'd travel more.	If he didn't earn so much, he wouldn't spend so much.
He'd understand the reason if you explained it.	I wouldn't invest in that company if I were you.

Question	Short answers
Would you stop work if you won £1 million?	Yes, I would.
Would he work abroad if he got the chance?	No, he wouldn't.
If you had six months off work, how would you spend the time?	—

Use	Examples
Unlikely or unreal situations and their probable results	*If public transport were free, there would be fewer cars in the city centres.*
	If I were the Transport Minister, I would increase petrol prices.

- The *if* clause can come before or after the main clause. When the *if* clause comes first, we usually put a comma between it and the main clause.
  If I won a lot of money, I'd buy a Ferrari.
  I'd buy a Ferrari if I won a lot of money.

- With *I*, *he*, and *she*, we can use *was* instead of *were* in the *if* clause, especially in a more informal style.
  *If it **was** less expensive, he would buy it.*

- *Could* is both the Past and the Conditional of *can*.
  *When she lived in Paris, she **could visit** the Louvre at any time.* (Past)
  *We **could make** some of the money if we charged motorists.* (Conditional)

- The Past tense does not refer to past time in a conditional sentence. It refers to an unreal situation.
  *If I **were** the Transport Minister,...* (but I'm not).

Modal verbs

can could may might shall should will would must mustn't needn't

Modal verbs add extra meaning to the main verb.

Use	Examples	Use	Examples
Necessity	He **must** have a visa.	Permission	**Can** I use your phone?
Prohibition	They **mustn't** leave without paying.		**Could** I interrupt you for a moment? **May** I borrow your car?
No necessity	You **needn't** make an appointment.	Ability	**Can** you speak Spanish? She **could** swim when she was three.
Advice	You **should** always be punctual. You **shouldn't** use first names.	Requests	**Could** you repeat that, please? **Will** you post this letter for me? **Would** you type this letter, please?
Possibility	Paperwork **can** take a long time. Your host **may** invite you to his home. I **might** be late.	Offers	**Would** you like a drink? **Shall** I call a taxi for you?

- The form of a modal verb is the same for all persons. We don't add *-s* to the 3rd person singular of a modal verb.
  I/You/He/She/It/We/They **may** *arrive late.*
  He **can** *speak German.*

- We don't use *to* after modal verbs.
  I must ~~to~~ go now.

- To make the negative of a modal verb, we add *not* or *n't*. We don't use *don't* and *doesn't*.
  He **can't**/**cannot** *speak Japanese.*
  You **mustn't**/**must not** *drive on the right in the UK.*
  She **may not** *arrive before you leave.*

- We can't add *-n't* to *may*.
  She ~~mayn't~~ arrive before you leave.

- We put the modal verb before *I/you/he*, etc. to make a question.
  Should *I confirm the booking by letter?*

- With *I* and *we*, we use *shall* for offers, and when asking for and making suggestions.
  Shall *I close the door?*
  What **shall** *we do?*
  Shall *we go to the park?*

- We can use *have to* for necessity.
  I **have to** *work overtime sometimes.*
  We can use *don't have to* when there is no necessity.
  I **don't have to** *work on Saturdays.*

The Passive

be (is/was/have been, etc.) + past participle *(produced/built/grown,* etc.)	
Positive	Negative
Coffee **is grown** in Brazil. The company **was founded** in 1970. Vines **have been grown** in this area for over 2,000 years.	Cigarette advertising **isn't allowed** in cinemas. Prices **weren't increased** last year. A decision **hasn't been made** yet.

Question	Short answer
Are Peugeot cars **made** in France?	Yes, they **are**.
Were the goods **delivered** on time?	No, they **weren't**.
Has the factory **been built** yet?	Yes, it **has**.
How **is** champagne **produced**?	—
When **will** it **be finished**?	—
How long **has** this method **been used**?	—

We use the Passive when the person or thing that does the action isn't important, or when we don't know who does it. If we want to say who does or did the action we use *by*.

Active

*The architect IM Pei **designed** the Louvre Pyramid in Paris.*

Passive

*The Louvre Pyramid in Paris **was designed** by IM Pei.*

Prepositions of time

in
- **month/season/year/century**
  June
  winter
  1996
  the 21st century

- **part of the day**
  the morning
  the afternoon
  the evening

at
- **time/meal time**
  six o'clock
  lunch time
  midnight

on
- **day/date**
  Tuesday
  6 December
  Easter Monday
  Christmas Day
  Friday morning
  Wednesday evenings

at
- **period of two or three days**
  the weekend
  Christmas
  Easter

Prepositions of place and direction

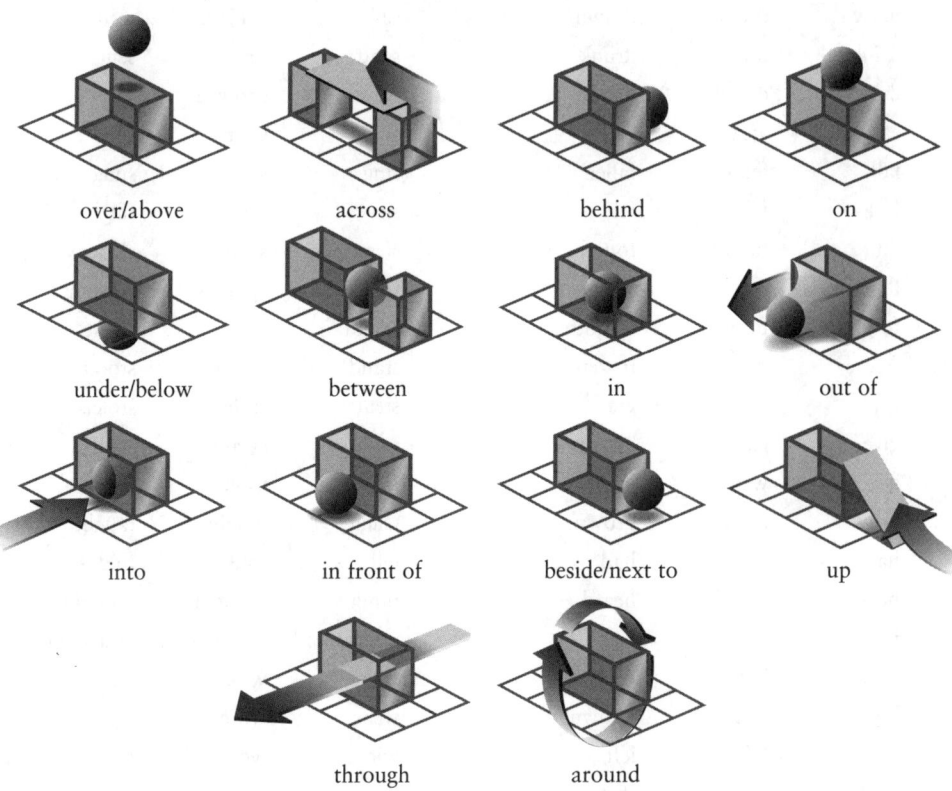

over/above · across · behind · on

under/below · between · in · out of

into · in front of · beside/next to · up

through · around

Irregular verbs

Infinitive	Past	Participle	Infinitive	Past	Participle
be	was/were	been	lose	lost	lost
become	became	become	make	made	made
begin	began	begun	mean	meant	meant
break	broke	broken	meet	met	met
bring	brought	brought	pay	paid	paid
build	built	built	put	put	put
buy	bought	bought	read	read	read
catch	caught	caught	ride	rode	ridden
choose	chose	chosen	ring	rang	rung
come	came	come	rise	rose	risen
cost	cost	cost	run	ran	run
cut	cut	cut	say	said	said
do	did	done	see	saw	seen
draw	drew	drawn	sell	sold	sold
drink	drank	drunk	send	sent	sent
drive	drove	driven	show	showed	shown
eat	ate	eaten	shut	shut	shut
fall	fell	fallen	sing	sang	sung
feel	felt	felt	sit	sat	sat
find	found	found	sleep	slept	slept
fly	flew	flown	speak	spoke	spoken
forget	forgot	forgotten	spend	spent	spent
freeze	froze	frozen	stand	stood	stood
get	got	got	steal	stole	stolen
give	gave	given	swim	swam	swum
go	went	gone	take	took	taken
grow	grew	grown	teach	taught	taught
have	had	had	tell	told	told
hear	heard	heard	think	thought	thought
hit	hit	hit	understand	understood	understood
keep	kept	kept	wake	woke	woken
know	knew	known	wear	wore	worn
leave	left	left	win	won	won
lend	lent	lent	write	wrote	written

SOCIAL ENGLISH

Meeting people

Introductions

May | I introduce myself?　　My name's... (*James Turner*).
Can |　　　　　　　　　　　I'm... (*Monique Bresson*).

May | I introduce a good friend of mine? This is... (*Roberto Angelini*).
Can |

Excuse me, are you... (*Duncan Ross*)?
Hello, you must be... (*Luigi Bastini*).

I'd like to | introduce you to... (*Tony White*).
Let me |

> How do you do.　　　　　→ How do you do.
> Pleased to meet you.　　→ Pleased to meet you, too.
> Please call me... (*Luigi*). → Then you must call me... (*Monique*).

Greetings

Hello,... (*Roberto*).

Good | to see you again.
Nice |

> How are you?　　→ Fine, thanks. And you?
> How are things?　→ Not too bad, thanks.
> How's the family? → Very well, thank you.

　　　| morning.
Good | afternoon.
　　　| evening.

● We only say *Good night* when we are leaving. We don't use it as a greeting.

Goodbyes

I must go now.
We really must leave now.
I must be off.

> It was very nice meeting you. → I really enjoyed meeting you, too.
> Have a good | trip.　　　→ Thank you... (*and the same to you*).
> 　　　　　　| journey.
> 　　　　　　| flight.
> I hope to see you again. → I hope so, too.

I look forward to... (*seeing you again*).
I'm looking forward to... (*our next meeting*).

See you | on the... (*1 July*).　　　Have a good | trip back.
　　　　| next week.　　　　　　　　　　　　　| flight back.
　　　　| soon.

17

Telephoning

Making contact
Hello. This is... (*James Turner*).

> Is that... (*Monique Bresson*)? → Yes, speaking.
> I'd like to speak to... (*Mr Brown*). → Who's calling, please?
> Could I speak to... (*Manfred Weiss*)? → May I know who's calling, please?

I'm calling about... (*the letter I sent you*).

Hold the line, please.

I'm sorry... | (*Mr Weiss*) is in a meeting at the moment.
I'm afraid... | (*he*)'s busy at present.
             (*she*) isn't here.

Leaving a message
Can I | take a message?
       leave a message?

Could you take a message?

Could you | ask... (*her*) to call... (*Luigi Bastini*)?
              tell... (*him*) that... (*Duncan Ross*) called?

Could you spell... (*your name*), please?
What's your number, please?

Welcoming a visitor

The journey here
Did you have a good journey?
How was your flight?
Did you have any problems finding us?
How did you get here?
Are you here on business?

Work
What do you do?
Where do you work?
What are you working on currently?

The weather
What was the weather like in... (*London*)?

Travel and holidays
Do you travel a lot?
Which countries do you visit?
Where did you spend... (*your last holiday*)?

The visitor
Where do you live?
Which part of the country/city is that?

First impressions
What do you think of... (*the new airport*)?
Is this your first visit to... (*Barcelona*)?
How long are you here for?

Sports and leisure
What do you do at the weekends?
Do you play any sports?

News
What's the latest news on... (*the election*)?
Is there any news about... (*the conference*)?

Staying at a hotel

Booking a hotel
I'd like to book a | single room for 4 April.
 | double

Arriving at a hotel
I have a reservation.

Making requests
I'd like a room, please.
Could I have an early morning call, at 6.30?
Could I have my bill, please?
Can I pay by credit card?

At a restaurant

Recommending
What do you recommend?
The... (*seafood*) is usually excellent here.
I recommend the... (*chicken*).

Ordering
I'll | have... (*smoked Scottish salmon*).
We'll |

I'd | like... (*the roast Normandy pork*).
We'd |

Could we have... (*a bottle of mineral water*)?

Offering
Do have some more... (*prawns*).
What about... (*dessert*)?
How about... (*some strawberries*)?
Would you like... (*a coffee*)?

Accepting
Yes, I'd like that.
Yes, that would be very nice.

Declining
Thank you, but I couldn't eat any more.
No, thank you.

Thanking and responding

Thank you for a really excellent meal. →	Don't mention it.
Thank you for a lovely evening. →	I enjoyed it very much, too.

Making arrangements

Making an appointment

When	would be convenient for you?
What time	could we meet?
	are you free?
	would suit you?

Shall we say... *(next Tuesday)*? → Yes,... *(Tuesday)* suits me fine.
Is... *(9.30)* possible for you? → Yes, that's fine.
How about... *(Friday)*? → Yes, I can make it on... *(Friday)*.
What about... *(the afternoon)*? → No, I'm afraid I'm busy then.
Could we arrange... *(to have lunch)*? → No, I'm afraid I've got another appointment then.

I look forward to meeting you on... *(Wednesday)*.
See you... *(next week)*.

Changing an appointment
I'm very sorry I have to cancel the appointment on... *(Friday)*.
I'm afraid I can't manage our meeting... *(tomorrow)*.
Could we arrange another time?

Opinions and suggestions

Asking for opinions
What do you think about... *(the design)*?
What's your opinion of... *(the quality)*?
How do you feel about... *(the price)*?

Giving opinions
In my opinion... *(it's excellent)*.
I think... *(it's rather expensive)*.

Agreeing
I agree.
I certainly agree with that.
I agree completely.

Disagreeing
I'm afraid I don't agree.
I'm sorry, but I disagree.

Asking for suggestions
Do you have any suggestions for... *(the agenda)*?
Any ideas on... *(the parking problem)*?

Making suggestions
I suggest... *(we meet at the hotel)*.
How about... *(going by plane)*?
What about... *(giving a talk)*?
Why don't we... *(have a meeting)*?
Why not... *(finish with a party)*?
We could... *(arrange a tennis tournament)*.

Accepting suggestions
Yes, that's a good idea.
Yes, let's do that.

Rejecting suggestions
Yes, but... *(it's too far away)*.
I'm not sure about that.
I'm afraid I don't like that idea.

Invitations

Inviting

I'd like to invite you to... (*have dinner with me*).
Would you join us... (*for a game of tennis*)?
Would you like to... (*come swimming*)?
Why don't you... (*have lunch with us*)?
How about... (*joining us*)?

Accepting

Thank you. I'm delighted to accept.
Thank you. I'd love to.
Thank you. I'd enjoy that.

Declining

I'd love to, but... (*I'm afraid I can't*).
Thanks a lot but... (*I've made another arrangement*).

Offers and Requests

Offering

Shall I... (*open the window*)?
Do you want me to... (*post the letter for you*)?
If you like, I can... (*give you some help*).

Would you like me to... (*arrange a meeting*)?

Accepting

Yes, please.
Thank you.
That's very kind of you.
Thank you. I'd appreciate that.

Declining

Thanks, but please don't bother.
Thanks, but that won't be necessary.
That's very kind of you, but... (*I can manage*).

Requesting

Can you... (*come tomorrow*)?
Could you... (*write her a letter*)?
Would you... (*book the hotel*)?
Do you think you could... (*check it*)?

Would you mind... (*checking it*)?
Do you mind... (*checking it*)?

Agreeing

Yes, of course.
Yes, certainly.

Not at all.
No, of course not.

Refusing

I think that will be difficult... (*There isn't enough time*).
I'm afraid not... (*I'm very busy*).
I'm sorry, but that's not possible... (*I'm leaving now*).
I'm afraid not.

Asking for information

Asking
I'd like some information about... (*flights to Paris*).
I'd like to know... (*how long it takes*).
Do you know... (*when the train arrives*)?
Can | you tell me... (*how often the trains leave*)?
Could|

Showing understanding
I see.
Right, I've got that.
So,... (*the next train's in half an hour*).

Asking for repetition
Could you repeat that, please?
Could you say that again?

Checking
Let me check.
I'll look that up.

Apologizing
I'm afraid I don't have any information about... (*domestic flights*).

Social responses

Thanking
Thanks for all your help.	→	Don't mention it.
Thank you for your advice.		Not at all.
		You're welcome. (US)

Apologizing
Sorry I'm late.	→	It doesn't matter.
I'm sorry. I've broken a glass.		Don't worry.
		Never mind.

Asking for repetition
Sorry?
Pardon?
Could you repeat that, please?
I'm sorry, I didn't catch... (*your name*).

Asking and giving permission
May I sit here?		Yes, of course.
Could I use your phone?	→	Please do.
		Yes, certainly.
Do you mind if I open the window?	→	No, not at all.

Refusing permission
| Could I borrow your car? | → | Sorry, but I need it. |
| Do you mind if I smoke? | → | Well, I'd rather you didn't. |

Giving and passing things
| Have you got the tickets? | → | Yes, here they are. |
| Could you pass the bread, please? | → | Yes, here you are. |

Expressing surprise

| They've got six children now. | → | Really! |

Responding to good news

| I've passed my final exams! | → | Congratulations!
That's great! |

Responding to bad news

| I failed my driving test. | → | Oh, I'm sorry to hear that. |

Responding to good wishes

| Have a good weekend. | → | Thanks. You too. |
| I hope you enjoy your holiday. | → | Thanks, and the same to you. |

Saying goodbye

Thanking for hospitality

Thank you | for inviting us.
          | for everything.
          | very much for your hospitality.
Thanks a lot.

We've had a wonderful time.
It was really enjoyable.
I really appreciated it.
Everything was great.

Responding to thanks

I'm glad you | could come.
             | enjoyed it.
             | found it interesting.
             | liked it.

Asking for help

Sorry, I don't understand.
I don't know what... ('*currently*') means.
What does... ('*working knowledge*') mean?
What do you call this in English?
How do you say... ('*Je voudrais une chambre*') in English?
Could you say that again, please?
Could you repeat that, please?
Could you speak more slowly, please?
Could you spell that, please?
Could you write that down, please?

Other Useful Information

Business correspondence

CUNNINGHAM ASSOCIATES
26, Trent Rd, Bicester, Oxon OX6 8RN
Tel: 0869 204950 Fax: 0869 204900

22 February 1996

Jean Paul Leclerc
ZigZag SA
74, rue Jules Ferry
75116 Paris

Dear Mr Leclerc[1]

Thank you for your letter of 15 January.[2] I apologize for not replying sooner.[3]

I am writing to inform you that I am coming to Paris on 7 March.[4] I would be delighted to meet you to discuss the fashion show, as you suggested.[5] Unfortunately, as I am flying to Rome in the afternoon, I will not be able to visit your factory, and cannot attend your company dinner in the evening.[6]

I would be grateful if you could send me your catalogue and price list as soon as possible, as I would like to show your Summer Collection to the fashion buyers at our monthly meeting next week.[7]

I am enclosing a copy of an excellent magazine article about fashion retailers in this country. I hope you find it interesting.[8]

I look forward to meeting you next month.[9] Please let me know if you would like any further information.[10]

Yours sincerely[11]

David Cunningham

David Cunningham
Manager

Opening[1]   (See also **Closing** [11].)

Dear | Sir
     | Madam
     | Mr Murphy
     | Mrs Hobbs
     | Miss Young
     | Ms White
     | George
     | Dr Green

- When you don't know the receiver's name, use *Sir* or *Madam*.
  For a man, use the receiver's family name with *Mr*.
  For a married woman, use the receiver's family name with *Mrs* or *Ms*.
  For an unmarried woman, use the receiver's family name with *Miss* or *Ms*.
  For a close business contact or friend, use the receiver's first name.
  For a doctor, use *Dr* and the family name.

- *Ms* can replace *Mrs* and *Miss*. It doesn't indicate whether a woman is married.

Making reference[2]
Thank you for	*your telephone call today.*
With reference to	*your letter of 8 January,...*
Further to	*your letter of 30 August,...*

Apologizing[3]
I apologize for	*the delay.*
	not replying sooner.

I am sorry that I am not able to help you.

Explaining the reason for writing[4]
	ask you...
I am writing to	*enquire about...*
	inform you that...
	confirm...

Agreeing to requests[5]
I would be	*delighted to...*
	pleased to...

Giving bad news[6]
I am afraid that...
Unfortunately,...

Requesting[7]
I would be grateful if you could...
We would appreciate it if you could...
Could you possibly...?

Enclosing documents[8]
I have pleasure in enclosing...
I am enclosing...
I enclose...

Referring to future contact[9]
	meeting you next month.
I look forward to	*receiving your reply.*
	hearing from you soon.

Finishing[10]
Please let me know if	*you have any questions.*
Please contact us again if	*we can help in any way.*
	you would like further information.

Closing[11]   (See **Opening**[1])
Yours	*faithfully*
	sincerely

Best wishes

- When you open the letter with *Dear Sir* or *Dear Madam*, use *Yours faithfully*.
  When you open the letter with the receiver's family name, use *Yours sincerely*.
  For a close business contact or friend, use *Best wishes*.

American English

This section describes some differences between American and British English. The differences are not very great, and they may vary between regions across the USA.

have/have got
To express possession, British people often say *have got*.

British	British/American
I've got a German car.	I have an Italian car.
Have you got a fax machine? Yes, I have. No, I haven't.	Do you have any children? Yes, I do. No, I don't.

The difference is only in the Present Simple. There is no difference in other tenses.

When we use the verb *have* for an action, there is no difference between American and British English.

British/American
I have an English lesson every week.
Do you have coffee for breakfast?   Yes, I do.
                                    No, I don't.

Present Perfect/Past Simple
Where British English uses the Present Perfect, American English often uses the Past Simple.

British	American
I've just finished the report.	I just finished the report.
Have you seen her yet?	Did you see her yet?
I haven't finished the work yet.	I didn't finish the work yet.
We've already met.	We already met.

Prepositions

British	American
at the weekend	on the weekend
five minutes past two	five minutes past/after two
ten minutes to six	ten minutes to/of six
write to me	write me
meet someone	meet with someone
stay at home	stay home
Tuesday to Saturday	Tuesday through Saturday
visit somebody	visit with somebody

Dates (written)

British	American
2.11.94 2 November 1994	11/2/94 November 2 1994

Dates (spoken)

British	American
She started work on the second of November, nineteen ninety-four.	She started work on November second, nineteen ninety-four.

Vocabulary

British	American
flat	apartment
car	automobile
taxi	cab
chemist's	drug store
lift	elevator
autumn	fall
tap	faucet
ground floor	first floor
motorway	freeway
petrol	gas
post	mail
cinema	movie theater
trousers	pants
wallet	pocketbook
railway	railroad
toilet	rest room
return ticket	round trip ticket
pavement	sidewalk
tube/underground	subway
holiday	vacation

Mathematical terms

+	$3 + 5 = 8$	three *plus* five is eight
−	$7 - 1 = 6$	seven *minus* one is six
÷	$20 \div 2 = 10$	twenty *divided by* two is ten
×	$3 \times 3 = 9$	three *times/multiplied by* three is nine
=	$1 + 4 = 5$	one plus four *is/equals* five
%	75%	seventy five *per cent*
	$1/4$	a quarter
	$1/3$	a third
	$1/2$	a half
	$3/4$	three quarters
	$1\tfrac{1}{2}$	one and a half

Countries and nationalities

Country	Nationality	Country	Nationality
America (the USA)	American	India	Indian
Australia	Australian	Ireland	Irish
Austria	Austrian	Italy	Italian
Belgium	Belgian	Japan	Japanese
Brazil	Brazilian	the Netherlands	Dutch
Canada	Canadian	Norway	Norwegian
China	Chinese	Poland	Polish
the Czech Republic	Czech	Portugal	Portuguese
Denmark	Danish	Romania	Romanian
Finland	Finnish	Russia	Russian
France	French	Slovakia	Slovak
Germany	German	Spain	Spanish
Great Britain (the UK)	British	Sweden	Swedish
Greece	Greek	Switzerland	Swiss
Hungary	Hungarian	Turkey	Turkish

Phonetic symbols

Vowels

iː	as in	see /siː/	u	as in	situation /ˌsɪtʃuˈeɪʃn/
ɪ	as in	sit /sɪt/	ɜː	as in	fur /fɜː(r)/
e	as in	ten /ten/	ə	as in	ago /əˈgəʊ/
æ	as in	hat /hæt/	eɪ	as in	page /peɪdʒ/
ɑː	as in	arm /ɑːm/	əʊ	as in	home /həʊm/
ɒ	as in	got /gɒt/	aɪ	as in	five /faɪv/
ɔː	as in	saw /sɔː/	aʊ	as in	now /naʊ/
ʊ	as in	put /pʊt/	ɔɪ	as in	join /dʒɔɪn/
uː	as in	too /tuː/	ɪə	as in	near /nɪə(r)/
ʌ	as in	cup /kʌp/	eə	as in	hair /heə(r)/
i	as in	happy /ˈhæpi/	ʊə	as in	pure /pjʊə(r)/

Consonants

p	as in	pen /pen/	s	as in	so /səʊ/
b	as in	bad /bæd/	z	as in	zoo /zuː/
t	as in	tea /tiː/	ʃ	as in	she /ʃiː/
d	as in	did /dɪd/	ʒ	as in	vision /ˈvɪʒn/
k	as in	cat /kæt/	h	as in	how /haʊ/
g	as in	got /gɒt/	m	as in	man /mæn/
tʃ	as in	chin /tʃɪn/	n	as in	no /nəʊ/
dʒ	as in	June /dʒuːn/	ŋ	as in	sing /sɪŋ/
f	as in	fall /fɔːl/	l	as in	leg /leg/
v	as in	voice /vɔɪs/	r	as in	red /red/
θ	as in	thin /θɪn/	j	as in	yes /jes/
ð	as in	then /ðen/	w	as in	wet /wet/

Grammar timelines

Past Simple

Present Perfect Simple

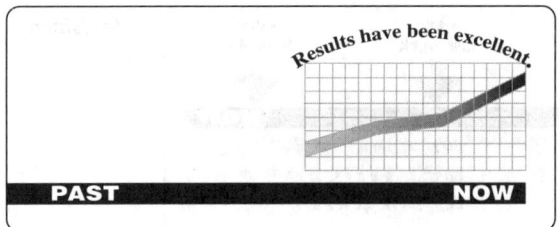

Present Perfect Simple

Grammar timelines

Present Perfect Simple with *ever*

Present Perfect Continuous

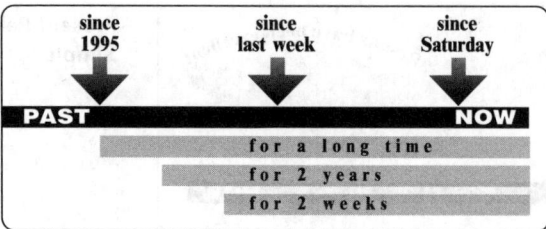

for/since